Spotli
Poets

Seated In The Soul

Edited by Sarah Marshall

Spotlight
Poets

First published in Great Britain in 2005 by
SPOTLIGHT POETS
Remus House
Coltsfoot Drive
Peterborough
PE2 9JX
Telephone: (01733) 898102
Fax: (01733) 313524
Website: www.forwardpress.co.uk

SB ISBN 1 84077 146 1

Foreword

As a nation of poetry writers and lovers, many of us are still surprisingly reluctant to go out and actually buy the books we cherish so much. Often when searching out the work of newer and less known authors it becomes a near impossible mission to track down the sort of books you require. In an effort to break away from the endless clutter of seemingly unrelated poems from authors we know nothing or little about; Spotlight Poets has opened up a doorway to something quite special.

Seated In The Soul is a collection of poems to be cherished forever; featuring the work of twelve captivating poets each with a selection of their very best work. Placing that alongside their own personal profile gives a complete feel for the way each author works, allowing for a clearer idea of the true feelings and reasoning behind the poems.

The poems and poets have been chosen and presented in a complementary anthology that offers a variety of ideals and ideas, capable of moving the heart, mind and soul of the reader.

Sarah Marshall

Contents

Beryl Dobson 43

Julie Walker-Daniel 59

The Authors
& Poems

Janis Mackay

I come from Edinburgh, Scotland. Having nurtured dreams of 'being a writer' since early childhood, I thought journalism sounded like a good idea. I trained as a journalist, worked in Fleet Street but by the age of twenty-two was disillusioned and gave this up to see the world and seek a more poetic life! Always interested in language I trained in speech and drama and have been working for several years as a voice coach, performance poet, actress and storyteller. The dream of writing though was never far away and I took an MA in creative writing and personal development at the University of Sussex. Now, together with my speech teaching, I also teach creative writing and, after many years of performing poetry and speaking other poets' words, I am now finding my own voice as a writer.

I write poetry, much of it inspired by the land, by family, by sense of place, belonging - or displacement. For me a poem is often born out of something I am told, a snippet of a story, or something I see in the landscape. For me the activity of writing is one where I aim to connect with my Self, to my deeper truth and my story.

As I write I have a sense (when it goes well) of knitting myself into the fabric of life - my way of finding my place and giving something of myself to the community. In this sense poetry feels like a communion. The land is synonymous with the body and in my poetry I explore a sense of belonging in one's body, also of taking back. I see that the act of writing can help us to reclaim what is ours. As a poet I am inspired by sound and write for a sense of how the poem will sound spoken.

Scotland, the land, language, her people, wild spirit, history and identity has a great influence on my writing. I am inspired by writers like W B Yeats, Norman Macaig, Don Paterson, Elizabeth Bishop, G M Hopkins, W H Auden, Mary Oliver, Eavan Boland and many others. I am interested in poetry's ability to reach out, communicate, inspire and to make whole.

An Imaginary Painting

A woman sits in the lamplight
Her head bent over a china bowl,
Her eyes closed.
She's still half-dreaming.

Her thick ginger hair has been down
Skirting all night, now strands fall
Over a face we'd call plain, but then
Men found that puffed paleness beautiful.

The lamp gives off an amber light
And the whiff of paraffin
She'll cover later with lavender oil,
Into cold water she'll waken

And the hard pillow lines of sleep
Will lift out of her pinking cheek
Or so I imagine it might have been
When women washed in bowls at dawn,

And lamplight smelled. Face creams
Have not been invented yet,
But she has inherited tricks for beauty
Like handstands for shining eyes

Pinching for rosiness
Biting for plump red lips
Smiling for lines going kind ways
And singing for a lilt in speech.

As looking glasses are rare and tainted
This woman belongs to herself.
She feels good in her skin
At home in her beauty. Whole within.

Married

I'm into domesticity
Oh babe, do I ever dig it?
Just catch me doing nothin'
No way, I'm right there in it
Up tae ma elbows
In hot soapy bubbles
And if it's no greasy crockery
It's his cute stained jocks - hell
I find the whole thing thrilling,
Cos I'm into domesticity
I'm not yer average housewife
For one ma name's *Finula*
Come frae Ladybank in Fife - oh
I'm scrubbin'
Moppin'
Spongin'
Shoppin'
Bakin'
Takin' time tae cook his dinner
An' I do it wi' a smile
Wi' a song, wi' ma . . . sussies on,
A cheery wave tae the milkie
Wee wave fir the postie
A 'Nice day eh?' tae the checkout girl
Then it's home wi' ma messages,
Oh I'm into domesticity
Canny wait tae wash they winndaes!

Blackstock Road

The grimmest place was Blackstock Road, Finsbury Park.
I had the sofa,
Was 19.

When the girls, who would do anything to get on,
Had gone to their rooms
With chocolate Revels and vibrators

I watched the big knitted hatted men in doorways,
And the man in the bedsit above the Halal meat shop
Across the street.

I watched him take off his bloody overall;
And saw his pyjamas were underneath.
Neither of us had curtains.

Watching him climb into bed, I felt life
Fold up and rut
Into a few joyless yards

Shop below
Bed above
Air nowhere.

Did he come from wide eastern plains
To shrink the whole globe into this?
In the morning he put it on again - the blood.

Seeing him in that pink meat shop,
Cutting flesh, knowing he was ready for bed
The wretchedness fell into me

And I turned around
Caught the overnight bus from Victoria,
And left.

Forfeit

Then there are the places I carry inside;
The continents
                Countries
                        Cupboards
                                Cups
                                      And spoons.
Landlady me, I rent them out
For a fistful of coins
And keep to the roads I know.

But who has been drinking my wine?
Squatting?
Putting down weed killer,
                Up fences
                        Wearing my crown?

And why, when I had the world
Do I have no garden
Or home of my own?

Hmm!

Start
By retrieving the spoons.

Away Wi' Them

'It's Sunday today John, Sunday.'
John tells me he's away with the fairies
And tells me about the black holes in his brain.

Margaret tells him what he did,
Who he knows and doesn't,
And who the woman is in the painting
He started last year.

Her voice full of loved and stressed syllables
Her patience tested, 'No, it's January John, January.'
When it was just the deafness she spoke up
Now it's repeating - slowly - loudly

While the fairies are unpeeling onions
And he's right in the core
Weeping.

For his mother, not the drunken old bugger
Getting him up at midnight to sing, 'Ca' the Yowes.'
When the tears would stream down Father's cheek
Him swaying, pissed, and John's voice unbroken

Singing, 'I didnae go tae nae sic school
My father dear tae play the fool.'

Bonnie Dearie

The boys had been in bed for hours
half-sleeping, expecting him
One ear cocked,
Waiting for the door to clatter
The dim passage to echo,
For Mother's, 'No. Willie, no.'

For that rank night smell -
Chips, vinegar, and Father's 'Bells'.
For his lurching, hot breath in their room
His swaying in the shadow, squat, reeking
Pleading, 'Sing Ca' the Yowes, Johnnie,
Sing Ca' the Yowes.'

Then Johnnie would rise
Before the broken voice
To 'Ca' the Yowes, Tae the Knowes'
His voice high, beautiful
Father's salt-splashed cheeks,
His reeking, his sobbing,
'Guid Johnnie, guid.'
Years back.

Willie's long gone,
And John's eighty,
Can't remember what he did yesterday
But remembers singing 'Ca' the Yowes'
For the drunken old bugger.
Now it's Johnnie cries easy, breaks down
Thinking of Mother.
Bonnie dearie.

Salt From My Mother's Mother's Eyes

Johanna married William - or thought she did -
Then bore him four bastards,

Then married him again - sullenly -
Burning with shame
In a thin coat.

While Willie lied and drank
Her pride to the bone,
She lived by the kindred wisdom
Of having to lie
In the bed she made,

Told my mother (her one wedlocked issue), the same,
But she couldn't,
Nor have I,

These inherited beds were stained with shame.

At Duddingston Loch

It seemed then, so Sunday blest
With the swans, geese, reeds
And happy families in our bests,
Murmuring, tossing bread, laughing.

Watching at my mother's print dress
From the edge of the known world
This law of Sundays, bread crusts, webby swans,
Easter gold gorse and the clean smack of air.

I overheard their shuttered voices
Reckon the disused railway line
Beyond the Loch was,
'An awful rape and murder spot'.

And I knew, because we'd driven past
That just a tinker's walk away
Stood the corporation grey of Peffermill
Then Niddrie, then Craigmillar -

Where the poor people lived.
Where my mother had lived
Before she got away - now she stood
In her clean print dress, throwing bread,

The Standard Super Ten parked
At the entrance to Arthur's Seat,
And back in the white bungalow
A chicken spitting in the oven.

Over the Loch, brown and dust-white reeds
Waved to us in the April sun
While I ate the crusts
Meant for the wild.

Camusdarach My Jo

Skye, Eigg and Rhum are sun-basked,
Then gone, then soaked grey scunnered
Under riots of black banshee rain,

We shelter from the teeth of the wind
Wonder at the gull's muster
And hug into the rock's face.

Under us sprigs of wiry heather
Blushed moss, russet wind-broken bracken,
Everywhere grace and the gowan's fine.

Wind-lashed we dash to the hill's crown
Look down to the breaking white green
Black cracked glistening sea.

On over to snow-hooded mountaintops
Clustered like brooding Druids
Round the dark quiet of Loch Shiel.

Then a dram of amber from a break in the sky
Drawn sudden, saying here's to the sound of Arisaig
Rolling in like cream gold velvet over Camusdarach sands.

Slainte!

Gaelic And The Bagpipes

The great piper's seated in his kitchen,
Where the heart's ripped out,
The mother tongue's stung,
And he's blowing the beast to life.

Blows so there'll be less forgetting,
So there'll be a nation stirring,
A raw and ancient skirling
And spines that wing.

His eyes close as formica and microwave
Become range, peat and flame,
And the word 'suit' that fits ill, loosens
Into the ancient speech that knits and lilts,

Easing the shame that after five centuries
There's not a Macdonald left in Glenuig,
And the ancestral Highland seat's
A refuge from his flat in Leith.

When the new year's in,
He'll leave Moidart to teach the city
Gaelic and the bagpipes,
Where people photograph him,

Even us, even here,
We snap, catch the beast in his kitchen
While the spirit, too tethered,
Is slipping away.

Highland Fling

('There is only one thing that is certain; everything changes' I Ching)

This south-westerly combing Camusdarrach's
Out to whet you.

The glass-smooth sea of yesterday
Is broody, broken and clawing at rocks
As though to say;
Like this
Live
Let go

Gull bright tide cry
Out
Cry in
Salt nip spray fling

Trust
Dive
Swim

Glenuig Song

I saw a stag antlered in the glen
I saw a hind, motionless and then
I saw the night fall upon the fields
A thousand stars, black and silver seals.

I heard a gull cry to the lashing tide
I heard the waves break like a taken bride
I heard you sing, though sure you were not there
Then willed that flesh form in the salt-fresh air.

Jesus In Peckham Rye

His suit was sharp. From the Heart Foundation.
He'd taken a few knocks, but wasn't complaining.
Wore a razor-short crew, and an Essex accent,
A knuckle tattoo, that He rubbed on her apples.
'Oi! Wanna touch, pay! Them's Golden Delicious.'
'I know,' He said. Then she started to tremble.
Fig leaf, earthquake, hot flush, gamble.
The market was packed. Her life was painful.
Too many dead. Her up at dawn selling apples.
And all He said was, 'I know.' She was on the ground crying.
He said it again, slow. And looked in her eyes.
Everyone she'd ever loved, they were there again.
He took her heart. And rubbed it till it glowed.
And this miracle, took all of eight seconds.
He gave her a tissue, she saw it was shining,
Then her eyes were opened, her ears glistened.
And that's when she heard Him. He was washing the rain.

Cuthbert Makwetura

I started writing poetry at high school as a hobby. I grew up quite lonely, without friends, and found escapism in poetry. I have been writing poetry ever since. My grandmother, Margaret Fletcher, is my guardian angel, always encouraging me and being there for me. She is a published poet and she did introduce to me a lot of overseas publishers, some of whom have managed to publish some of my works, Forward Press included.
I also do freelance writing for various local and international magazines. I am a member of the Association Of Freelance Writers.

In Harare, where I am based, I conduct and teach poetry classes for budding poets. Very soon I intend to go into big league writing and become a full-time writer.

Anyone who loves to write/read can contact me at cmakwetura@yahoo.co.uk.

After Rain

A beautiful sunrise after rain
View the countryside in a train
Of bough, leaf and sky
The forest full of animal laughter
Monkeys chirrup and chatter
The noise of water in the gutter
Like the noise of people in the ghetto
Air shrill with cicada songs
Weaver birds chat and gossip
A group of Christians pray and worship.

Fields ablaze with the sound of tractor engines
Sweet smell of wet soil turned by cultivators
I see African women in long dress
Backs bent to sow maize seeds
And soon, when the sun is hot
And all are tired
They go and sit under a shade
Cooling their burning throats with the traditional brew
Their strength regained anew.

Africa, My Beautiful Song

Africa, a giant elephant that lies still
The tropical climate doesn't chill
Landscape bisected by beautiful rivers and streams
The nights full of wonder and sweet dreams
The Nile River so startlingly wide and long
Ancient monuments full of mystery and silent beauty

In Johannesburg tasting Windhoek beer
And grilled elephant heart
In Kenya, chopping crabs and lobsters
Africa sing, Africa my beautiful song
Of bushmen painting on rock caves
Of monkeys shrieking in consternation
Of sand dunes in June in the Sahara desert
The marico sunbird sucking nectar
Animal farming so common, see all these hectares
Of burning animal skin and hooves
Of mud huts and grass-thatched roofs
In Zimbabwe viewing the beautiful countryside
Through binoculars on mountaintops and horseback
The game, a marvel to see
Of gemsbok, warthog and farmers' sjambok
In Lake Kariba, yachts and boats full
Of drunken tourists chanting African songs
Africa, a heaven on Earth.

Panorama Of Ontdekkers Park

Panorama of Ontdekkers Park
Sweet smell of aroma
Genesis of sunset
Stunning colour of roses
Voices, laughter and dance
Around the eye-catching Victoria Falls
The forest's animals chatter
The scenery, a magnificent chapter
Roses and lilies smile in glee
Kids cry and wee
Adults, absorbed, forget thee
Water arch in rainbow fountains
Mountains loom like a receding storm
Bees speak in hieroglyphics
Adults wine and dine
Children pantomime
Pine trees salute the breeze in kind
Under palmetto trees, bodies entwine
The bride rides the palomino
Piano music sweeter than wine
The glamour of Ontdekkers Park
Thrills like Eden park
Wild fruits glow with succulence
Water roars with turbulence.

Nature

Isn't it heaven to see such undulating green?
The forest ignited by nature's songs
Birds hop and mate on treetops
Giraffe nibble young leaves of crops
Striped zebras graze on dewy glades
Their teeth sharp like razorblades
The goods train sings its sad song *kwe kwe-e!*
Across the beautiful village of Kwe Kwe
Jersey cows, full of milk, obey nature and chew a cud
Calves, their limbs tall and features small like a tree bud
Dodge their mothers who cry *moo!*
Doves, amused, laugh, *coo!*
The herd boy dashes into the forest, his loo
The farmer nods and thinks it's cool

Love In The Rain

Two figures kissing in the rain
Their mouths searching, finding
A zigzag of forked lightning
Thunder hails his bolts
Feeling the fast-bird flutter of her heart
And the trembling warmth
Despair in his voice wanting more
Gasping and hands clasping

Soon they retreat into the large farmhouse
Their naked bodies casting fantastic dancing shadows
Against the hurricane lamplight
The sound of sex as the bed becomes talkative
Outside the rain falls with cataclysmic fury
Oh, Diana, I will love you forever!

St Valentine's Day

Darling, how beautiful the world
Is, seated with you on
That bay watching photogenic waterfalls
Dolphins and porpoises leaping in cheerfulness
Balloons in full flight
Across a clear blue sky
Fireworks of rose flowers exploding
Sky-high like a Roman candle
The snow in free fall
Darling, how beautiful you are
In my arms on this
St Valentine's Day
Hair ponytailed
Your outfit, a rose garden
Wearing a full moon smile
Nightingales hopping from one
Rosebush to another
Singing sweet love songs
Your eyes, big, round and glazing
Your full lips against mine
Taste sweeter than wine
My gift to you, a bouquet of roses
Oh, love's passion doses
Sinking on the bottomless
Pond of love this day
Love reduces us to mere kids
We forget our differences
And melt, with this lovely day.

Letter To Martha

My eyes shine bright
At the sight of you
Did I hear you correct
When you said you loved me?
I have read your letter twice
And thought it was new
I have seen a mermaid at sea
And thought it was you
Your beauty so eye-catching
Like a solar eclipse
Who else would I ever love
Other than you?
I am too lost in you
You are my heart's song
And make me abandon all the wrong
Forever I will love you.

Oh Sweet Love!

We lay side by side
Inert like animals in their habitat
Safe from the arrows of the hunter
Bodies entwined and drenched in perspiration
The moon, an enormous torch, guiding
She retreats into the depth of my arms
Seeking, finding
Moaning softly, begging for more
Her eyes half-closed
Drugged by love, o' sweet love!
The stars watching with their smiling eyes
Animals of the night coughing at a distance
Is this the small heaven you mentioned, Winnie
Where love, like a shark, swallowed Pinnie?

My Grandmother, Margaret Fletcher

Between ocean and blue sky
My grandmother and I
Where seagulls and angels fly
My grandmother, Margaret Fletcher
Cheerful like Anne of Green Gables
Entertains us with old hunting songs
And fascinating tales
Around a fireplace
Happy, sweet Grandmother.
My grandmother, Margaret Fletcher
In winter, dresses like a polar bear
Calls me, 'Dear,'
From Harare I say, 'Hello.'
My grandmother, Margaret Fletcher
Cheerful like Anne of Green Gables
Expert with her woollen cables
Crochets our jerseys
To keep us warm
From Johannesburg, Nicole says, 'Hello,'
Happy sweet Grandmother
My grandmother, Margaret Fletcher
Feeds us like little puppies
Our small tummies always tucked with food
She calls me 'Fatma'.
She drinks water from a mug
And greets us with a hug
Happy, sweet Grandmother.

God's Verdict, A Mountain Fall

The world, limp and bloated
In its orbit, bleeds of
Volcanic lava
Continents drift apart grudgingly
Like giant warships
The Earth, its future uncertain
Crippled by atomic bombs
And biological warfare
Man's idea of civilisation
Mangled bone, tortured flesh
Air stinks of human carcasses
Massacre after massacre
Even God in Heaven is in shock
To witness such evil from man
Of His flock
A man He once ago admired
And created in His own image
And bestowed to him all responsibility
A man now blinded by materialism
And bloodlust
Whose idea of Heaven is
His glamorous cities
God watches, but aloof
Only time will tell
And God's verdict
Will be a mountain fall
On the culprits involved.

Colour Me White

Lunchtime
The Devil's crunch time
Diver drown break dance
Driver frown dreadful glance
What's up Makwetura?
Oh, agony is my dragon.
How evil is the Devil
In Adam and Eve
At the Garden of Eden
Transforming the world, once Utopia
Into Ethiopia?
If God is white
And the Devil is black
Colour me white.
Doom is the planet of our existence
Hunger, anger, danger, not the endangered species
Paradise, the almost extinct zooed animal in Heaven
The polar regions live with no sunrise
Nor sunset
Gondwanaland explodes into pieces
The Eskimo freezes
Life in hospitals seizes
Volcano oozes
Blood oozes
The drunkard in escapism boozes
Oh the world bamboozles!

Sound Of Sleep

The sun has closed its eyelids
The entire Earth gone to sleep
Only the lonely wind is heard weep
The moon rises and guides
All creatures to their habitat
Mothers flanked by their young ones
The ocean looking magnificent
Under moonlight
Whales moo and somersault
Lovers caught by night take a break
Prepare a campfire
Share a joke in candlelight
Soon there is the sound of kissing
And the sound of sex
When night soothes them
There is the sound of sleep.

Twins

Tiny twins dumped by the riverside
One-day-olds with eyes still closed
Neatly wrapped in a basket
Their tiny legs kicking
Small hands knotted into fists
Are they demanding to know
Where their mother is?
A stray cow comes by, gives one look
Shakes her head in distaste
For she is a mother too
Only the River Lesabi is heard crying
A soft wind passes by and is heard muttering
Only the tree standing by watching
Knows where the devil their mother is.

He Shall Become Soil

A large group of people in Park Lane
With dusty, sweaty, red-rimmed eyes
Speaking in hushed tones
Picks and shovels hugging the men's shoulders
Wheelbarrows bearing rock boulders
Soon there is the sound of picks
Tearing through the hot dry earth
The coffin is soon lowered into earth
Accompanied by the shrill sound of wails
The coffin shall be covered with soil
God created him out of soil
When he dies, man shall become soil.

Beryl Dobson

Beryl Dobson is a housewife, now retired from a life in a wide variety of careers from tax officer to wages clerk to costing and purchasing clerk. She has three children and six grandchildren.

Her hobbies include sewing, reading, gardening and listening to music, both live and recorded. In her younger days she loved sports and in 1997 she ran the London Marathon for the 'Heart Foundation' raising £1360 in sponsorship.

Virtues

Prudence in our thoughts
Gentle reproofs, that be
Help us to struggle bravely on
And to conquer, adversity.

True perfection
Patience sublime
Will never be found
In a lifetime.

And vows we never break
Are as scarce
As ripples -
On a lake.

And the rosy hue of bliss, and peace
So forever, skyward
Like a flock of geese
To disappear
Amidst the mists of time.

Which?

If I could retrace my footsteps
Which volume would I unseal?
Which vision of delight
Would I reveal?

Which fadeless fancies
From life's tempestuous deep
Would I tenderly cherish
And forever want to keep?

And which radiant hours
And mysterios of joy
Would I wish to remain, immortal
For me to enjoy, which?

Books

A lot of my books are friends
The unspoken words, phrases and syllables
Are like music to my ears
Of enlightenment, as I read and read and read.

The passages and journeys, through the pages.
The adventures, the mystics and places.
The emotions of despair and solitude.
Of joy and wonderment,
Beguiling, in its entirety.

The interaction of the reader and author.
Delving into the unknown mixture
Of sentiment, and revelations
That may be surprising too.

Lost in thoughts,
Time stands still
Hold the last page,
I beckon at will!

If

If all the leaves were silver
And all the trees, were gold
And all the flowers were jewels
What a sight to behold!

And if all the stars were diamonds
A'twinkling in the sky
And all the clouds were - candyfloss
As they floated by.

And if all the snow was ice cream
And all the sea, was pop
And all the roundabouts went round and round
And the moon was a lollipop!

If!

Seeds Of Love

My love and I
Wish to seek a land
Where seeds of love
Do grow.

Where they'll be
Watered and nourished
And guarded,
Against each foe.

For me to enjoy
Liberty,
I must have freedom
In my love.

To have as long
As love can be
As the stars
May shine above

Somewhere

Somewhere in the sunlight shadows
Before the night beckons
And silence, throws a blanket
- All around

You might catch a glimpse
Of something, to cause wonderment.
Ah! It's nature's way
Of putting on a show -
Without a script.

And in the twilight
And the bleakness -
Of the enveloping night
The moon shines a spotlight
Down to the Earth.

And before the dawn chorus,
And the sun so bright,
Welcoming the flowers
As they, sway in the breeze
From moonbeam to sunbeam
Shall we dance?

Nightfall

When it's nightfall
And the world, is still
I think of you, my darling
And I always will.

And when the stars
Shine in the sky
It's the same, as my eyes
When they light on you.

And when the rain falls
It's like my tears
As when I think of you
And these empty years.

Ah! Nightfall, how swiftly
Does it come.
Now let me sleep,
For in my dreams, perhaps
I'll dwell again -
On your sweet and loving face.

You Can

You can take away
The stars, from up above
You can take away -
The moon,
That shines, on our love.

You can take away
The fishes - from the sea
But don't *ever*
Take away your love, from me.

You can take away
The warmth, from the sun
You can take away
The rivers, as they run.

You can take away
My daydreams, yes, every one
But, don't *ever,* no, *never*
Take away,
Your love from me.

You can take away
The trees - from the land
You can take away
Every grain of sand.

You can take away
The birds and the bees.
But, don't *ever,* no, *never*
Take away,
Your love from me.

Until

Until, I can no longer
Reach to touch you
Until, my love for you
Isn't strong
Until, I know
Within my heart
You don't belong.

Until, right is changed
To wrong
Until the memory of you
Is gone.

Until the sun
Ceases to shine
That's when I say
You're no longer mine.

Until the sea
Doesn't reach the shore
Until the rain
Ceases to pour

Until you say
'I don't love you
Anymore'
Until, until, until!

Wealth

What is wealth?
Priceless jewels, silver or gold?
Or is it -
Something else, perhaps
Something, you have and hold?

Well, my priceless jewels,
Are the dew-laden flowers,
And the stars, that shine at night
And *silver,* the silvery waves in the sea
And locks of hair, *silvery*-white.

The *gold,* the golden rays, of the sun
- A sun-drenched beach
Or a golden smile.

But the wealth I have
Is the wealth of knowledge
I've gathered and stored -
In the years.

To which I can add
Without any cost
As soon as the moment,
    -   *Appears!*

Call

Call my name 'Despair'
For *I* am *that*
When you're not there

Call my name 'Forgive'
For I'll do *that*
As long as I may live.

Call my name 'Lament'
For I am that
The day you *went.*

And call my name 'Happiness'
For I want no *other*
And nothing less!

Forever Fading

Ah! Sweet memories
Why are they so dim?
As I try to reach
To touch you
My head begins to swim.

Forever through the
Fading light
A memory breaks through
Now and then

And how I remember
Those golden hours
And dreams, we shared
Yes, but when?

It doesn't seem
So long ago
And yet, it seems
- So far.

Why can't it be,
As yesterday
And at,
That bewitching hour?

Heart Renderings

If yours is a doubting heart
Let your faith be strong
Because when faith is lost
Right seems to go, so wrong.

If yours be a desolate heart
Then no new emotion can you stir
For sad hearts grow weary
With every beat they incur.

But a happy heart
Is like a sunbeam
Majestic like the sun
Like some secret chord vibrating
And even work is such fun.

And in every hungry heart
Lie thoughts, closely entwined
Perhaps hungry for love,
And mysteries yet to find.

And a faithful heart
Where lies true love, and thoughtfulness
From sources, none may know
Silent and graceful,
With no outward show.

Silent Thoughts

The pattern of your beauty
With gracefulness is set
And your deep, dreamy eyes
Like mirrors
My innermost thoughts reflect.

And for a brief hour
I cannot forget
And I cherish you, in my mind
And also the day we met
Not known to all mankind.

For when the evening shadows lengthen
And the snowflakes
Of silence fall
May our love be as strong
As the stars are bright
And may I be your
Dream for *tonight.*

Constant

Like a candle that burns bright
So is my love - for you this night
And like the warmth from the flame
That's how my love is
Time and time again.

But if the candle, grows dimmer
My love will never just simmer
For it is constant and true
And always for you.

Julie Walker-Daniel

During the past two years my life has been on a roller coaster of happenings as my whirlwind affair with poetry came to the fore. I was lucky enough to get my first collection published with Anchor Books.

My book launch at the library was a success; since then I have been invited to read my poetry at various poetry readings, done several interviews for Yorkshire newspapers, Thomas Danby College and local radio.

Since the forming of 'The 21st Century Poets' in 2004, I have concentrated on the issues that look at drugs, crime and the effect on all our lives. My second collection is a mixture of rhyming and free verse poetry, so as to appeal to a wider audience.

Eventually, I hope to write novels but at the moment I am happy to continue with my poetry and study at Leeds University. I hope that the readers can find something which appeals to them within my work, as that is what makes it all worthwhile.

Life's Embers

The fireplace in the bedroom:
Such a beautiful sight;
I keep the curtains open
So that passers-by can share in its delight.
The flickering and the crackling
Drifting way into the night.

The fireplace in the bedroom:
Such a dreamy place to stare;
Memories, come back thick and fast
Swore I saw an old love but then again no.
Dozing off, then returning once more
Oh, if only we could.

The fireplace in the bedroom:
Such a wondrous place to stare;
I find myself dropping off my troubles there.
Keeping my toes warm and my heart aglow
Think I'll stay here forever
Because there is nowhere else I'd rather go.

My Haunted Heart

My God, you left your mark!
You spooned out my pride and ripped open my heart
Your torture comes and goes; dredges up my entire soul
Quietly and gently it cuts like a knife and all that jive.
My word! Your memory fleets back into my mind
Every now and then and even when I want to start again.
However, it's only for a while
Well right up until you crawl back from under the stone
You ascended from
Then you're gone, yet not for long . . .

My God, you left your mark!
You spooned out my pride and ripped open my heart.

Still Scared Of Ghosts

The returned spirits of another life
Fleeting memories but can still cut like a knife.
The remembered; coming back to a wide-opened wound
Pretending, because we were doomed.
The forgotten; floating back and forth into time
Reeling you in and playing havoc with your mind.
Maybe the past, the present and the future
Just happened to be one great big adventure.
Anyone who has ever cared will always be scared.
The ghosts of yesterday, don't go away, they disappear
Into the sphere, then finally and unexpectedly
Reappear.

All Hallows Eve

When Hallowe'en brings more than the demons
At your door!
When ghouls, ghosts and all it boasts arrives
At your door!
Remember that trick or treat is not so sweet
When hammering at your door,
When in the thick of night you get a fright
When hammering at your door
But for what it's worth, don't go near and never fear.
Remember that autumn's here so keep good cheer
And keep hammering on!

All Present And Correct

Don't ever go back to yesterday
Looking back fondly is just fine
But please don't break the chains of time, for they are there for a reason
Please stay away and make a fresh new season.
Let the past go:
Then there will be a brand new tomorrow.
The answers always lie in the present
Correct.

Poetry's Back In Vogue

(A tribute to W Shakespeare)

Dear Mr Shakespeare;

What would you say if you walked amongst us today?
Some might shout that you were slightly quaint
With your 'thee' and 'thou', 'oh' and 'how'! Alas:
Mr Shakes, I, for one, think you're swell.
Would you have your say on midsummer's day?
And would nothing compare and could you stand and stare?
Well, Sir, poetry is back in vogue; oh, Sir, I really do hope so.

Dear Mr Shakespeare;
What would you say if our centuries collided with your world?
Supposing that our Lennon met your King Lear, or Yoko
Met your Romeo. Alas, Bono's U2 met with the shrew
What would you do? Could you say what's done is done?
Mr Shakes, can you give us a break?
And what if the tempest strayed and the merchant of Venice
                                          just kept at bay
Or would you just say, that it's much ado about nothing?

Those Baker Boys

They danced in a dim-lit park
Whilst they ran with the mob, they would have to hurt some poor sod.
Then they became Baker boys
Whilst the streets are mean, that keeps them keen
But when the funds are low and nowhere to go
Then they meet their first blow.
All they will say is they just met a man, who held out a hand.
Shaved heads to get rid of the dregs
Silver-shone blades, yet held no escape.
The silent cries of the boys in the marketplace
Yet, it is replaced with laughter and anger
But not always in that order then
Like a lamb . . . to the slaughter
But if you held out your hand,
All they would say is that they just met a man
And he had to pay.

They dance in a dim-lit park
While they hold out their hand having become that man, then to
order
Back to the slaughter . . . like a lamb!

Take Me To Baywood

(A tribute to a bottle of 'red'
A tribute to my school friend, Angela, whose encouragement and
kindness will stay with me for the rest of my life)

Two old friends on one stolen afternoon
November had hit home, so all had become doom and gloom.
Yet, the Baywood once open became our refuge
Sipped and tasted we knew nothing would be wasted.
As the conversation progressed and the wine nice and neatly
Was to digest
Laughter flowed like that ruby red, placed upon my newly
Abandoned dusk.
Then tears took its place, and we released our thoughts,
Feelings and fears
Realising that it was not the first time in years, that we had talked
But as the Baywood ruby red glistened
We knew that it was the first time in years that we had really, truly
listened!
Hail the bottle of 'red' . . . take me to Baywood to ease my aching
head.

The Fox's Last Hunt

This vixen, did not always play things as straight as a die, but

As the race began, a young tender heart did pound
So a drum and a bugle played.
As the beat danced on to a familiar sound
So survival became a one-hit game.

As the race took place, a gentle confused heart did pound
So the enemy, picked upon your trail
As you knew full well, you were on uncertain ground
So sad, it even went beyond the pale

As the race lost faith, a fragile wounded heart did pound
So they had won, with a job well done
As for every king, a new queen, but we lost the fairest ever seen
So every fox must meet their hound

As the race finally over, a mended broken heart had stopped
Still, never silenced but allowed to enter home.
As a coated flag, draped and adorned, one of the finest that
they owned
Still, a tad too late, cunningly left to sleep in a well-done dome . . .
sorry, I mean a watery hole!

For the fox eventually had lost!

I Dreamed That I Danced

I danced up a dream and made it the finest
Ever seen.
I stored it big and kept it clean . . . oh yes I could
Be mean.

I kept it huge and didn't ever imagine what it would
Be like to lose.
I thought in technicolour, even turned the negative
From black to white.

Then it dissolved . . . but at least I dreamed that I danced
So I did.

Bells For The Innocent

As the child looked up from his desk
Knowing, the bell soon would ring
That damn bell.
As the others quickly rushed and pushed
The child, took his time.

As the child, thought about what awaited
When his day then would start.
That damn bell.
He wondered of his mother, *did she need*
His help? Sobering her up, his daily chore.

As the child, knew his father's moods off by heart.
Reading a poem, about daffodils, today in class
The other children clapped with glee.
It's hard to concentrate on such things.

When your life's in bits, a daffodil just won't do
Now a poppy with its seeds, might just apply.
The other children, their faces lit up
As the child, stared vacant at his empty exercise book.

Then the bell rang, damn!

Punishment Of The Pretty

A trained eye, a thin twist of a smile, seems to go
Unnoticed. However, the other kind cannot do their stuff
Without a second glance, but if second glances were chances
Then things would be more just, but it's not you see, it's the

Punishment of the pretty: the punishment of the pretty
Just time will tell; but please save your pity, as it's not over yet.

A tainted smile, a wink of an eye, watched closely
Uncharitable. However, the other kind, allowed to go behind
With a venom mind which matches their smiles, but bad eyes
Which look down and can slit leather.

Punishment of the pretty: the punishment of the pretty
Just time alone has told.

An Unforgotten Place

When love's first embrace took place
So solid that it rocked the box. Yet it's
Still there; but left with a shake of a hand
Empty and stark now, its promises echo
Around its walls. Quietly you reflect there

Where love's long last look, took place
So solid that it became a palace, but it's
now unfinished business - but a road
That you must travel. You'll see our ship
Forever placed in your memory . . . cheers

Two more friends like that and you won't
Need any more enemies, as you're locked
In a deep dark box, so silent is the night
Now we hold the key, and you must pay the price
Likewise. Yet again, you must await my return . . .

The Season For Kissing Frogs

The gigantic Christmas tree stood
In a bay window, for all the town
To see. Well, they saw alright, as
It was not that easy on the eyes.

Now the tree itself was sweet
It stood stout and adorned just the
Two colours, winter-red and silver
And smelt of peppermint Rennies.

The vulgar tree, did boast of flashing
Lights but no reality in sight.
Bombing around, little stone built
Streets, deep into the night like a crook . . . (I'm being kind).

Now, you're not the first nor the last, that I
Have left in a large empty house but
This pantomime's over, but still I will
Wrap up your cold ornamental lions

Because it's the season for kissing frogs.
One day you will meet your match who has not
Got a flashing tree or concrete lions, placed
Upon a hill. Forget the frogs and wait for the prince.

There is no reason, for kissing frogs even if it's the season.

Just Another

It's been and gone and already sung its song
Another cool - Yule, oh yes, we all played
The fool.

It's slipped us into the depth of winter, quietly
Whilst our minds occupied on fine wines
Well most of the time.

Its tinsel and turkey has lost its appeal
Here's wishing that egg and chips had been
Part of the deal.

It's slipped away but don't despair as the
Next one will not be long. Here once again
To sing its song.

The Rise Of The East

In a western waiting room queue, whilst
A busy receptionist did her best.
In the midst of the crowd stood a timid Asian
Woman,

Her dowdy black overcoat, wrapped tightly
Around her tiny little frame
In order to hide the golden silk and embroidered
Gaudy sari.

Her aim was to hide the shame, for not being
Right.

In her embarrassment, she kept her eyes cast
So as not to catch the glances,
In her vision that went from left to right, sunken and
Nothing.

Her chin, held so low that it touched her chest bone.
Feeling the pushes and hearing the whispers,
Her bones clenched, the queue joined forces, together
As one.

But then the receptionist recognised her, 'Doctor Hasseed,
Welcome to England!
Your surgery's down the corridor,' taking the Asian lady's
Dowdy coat.

Then the queue was astonished . . . so from right to left their
Eyes were cast,
So as not to catch her glances.

Two Ladies Seek

The high priestess of the eternal flame
Drunken on life's wearily wretched
Game,

Surrendered up the monthly blood
In favour of a selective inspiring
Glove.

Its velvet lustre seems to have gone
But still flourished trees and buds
Linger on,

As water cleanses their every vein
So begotten of a higher spiritual
Plane.

The priestess of the eternal flame
Given up, till the final birth of the
Earth mother's

Deadly game. To rock and rule in its heavenly duel.

The Caterpillar's Moon Song

As the inner struggle of this creature's
Bower, wakening towards its finest
Hour, silently it stretches, stripping
Its wretched wounds of old, upon
Life's stories forever told.

A shedding of youth if the moon lets go
And the silver girl has faced her woes.

As the outer shell, displays an awoken
Image of a broken spell, whispering,
Echoing and the ageing process gives
Up its final struggle. Christened once
More not by water but by fire.

A shaping up of a woman, finally the sun caught
And the gold lady, displays all that life has taught.

Sue Brooks

Born in Leicester on 16th July 1950 into a large family where money was scarce. I went to the local state schools and at the age of 11 attended New Parks Secondary Modern Girls' School in Leicester where I left at the age of 15, or should I say 14 because I left school two weeks before my 15th birthday to start work in a greetings card shop. At the age of 17 my love of animals took me to London to work with greyhounds for the National Racing Association. I did this work for six years until my marriage in 1973. Because my husband was a mobile civil servant I found myself moving to Somerset and then Hong Kong. We eventually moved to Scarborough in 1979.

I started to write poetry at the grand age of 48; it seems I woke up one morning and could not leave pen and paper alone. I work on a part-time basis as a holistic therapist and have written personal poems for many people over the years. I never fail to be amazed when stopped in the street a year or two later and thanked for the poem which they have kept to re-read if they need inspiration; one lady told me my verse is a better tonic than a glass of wine! It is comments like this that inspire me to write more poetry and, hopefully, one day reach out to many more people on a large scale.

My work has been published on numerous occasions by the local free newspaper, 'The Top Trader'; it has also appeared in the 'Pilgrim Healers Group UK' newsletter/booklet. My interests lie in 'Mind, Body and Soul' therapies. I love being in the countryside, it inspires me to write about the beauty surrounding us, I always take a pen and paper with me.

I have worked on a voluntary basis for 'Mind', the mental health charity so became interested in mental health issues, this inspired me to think about the emotional conflicts we can all go through within our mind, whether through stress or crisis etc. By helping at 'Mind' I have gained greater understanding of how thoughts can affect our feelings and bring about various worries and fears so we feel unable to cope with everyday life.

I hope my work inspires folk to . . . 'always look on the bright side of life' and not the sometimes, 'sad side of life'

Clouds

Clouds of white go floating by
Like large sailboats in the sky
The wind doth blow them across the sea
So all can see them wherever they may be
They travel to countries where others abide
We could compare them to that of the tide
For nothing is stationary on Mother Earth
God made it that way, His beauty is worth
Far more than money for this can bring strife
God's beauty does not, it only brings life
For the clouds, the sun, the sea and the surf
Make life worth living on Mother Earth
That which He places around us to view
If we look at it closely will give life anew
Each day is quite different like the clouds up above
He does this to show us how great is His love
He cherishes all placed on this Earth
And surrounds us in colour and beauty of worth
Giving life anew to every living thing
We should all give Him thanks and His praise we should sing.

Bored? Feeling Alone? Adopt A Family
To Call Your Own

No one need ever feel alone
Just adopt a family to call your own
If you do this, then you'll find life a joy
It will not matter whether girl or boy.

If your children have flown or have you now outgrown
Adopt a family to call your own
You can be aunt or uncle to a nephew or niece
Giving them such joy, and yourself inner peace.

If you're bored with the home and have no one for to care
Adopt a family, so you can share
Your time and your memories bringing in such a smile
Your new family will love them, making life so worthwhile.

So don't just sit there saying, 'There's no one to care.'
Just look around for laughter, it's bound to be there
There is always some poor mother, who's so worn and weary
Who would welcome the chance to have a friend who's not dreary.

You can take out the kids, you could have cups of tea
All problems become lighter, when children can run free
Your life could be full of fun, and the loneliness gone
By adopting a family you'll find life one long song.

My Child

The face of an angel
Hair of golden corn
A smile that dazzles
A star is born.

She shines like a star
Shedding light all around
Her smile is contagious
Her laughter abounds.

She brightens the day
With affection and love
Her giggles can be heard
By God up above.

Her nature is sweet
Her heart is so full
Her joy is contagious
A lesson to us all.

Thank God for this child
Who shines so bright
Infecting us all
With love and with light.

May we learn from my child
Sent from Heaven above
That life can be good
With laughter and love.

Bluebell Wood

A golden path where bluebells lay
Is cool and refreshing on a summer's day
The colour of blue and the soft breeze sound
Is where I lay so peace is found.

As I look up, the rays from the sun
Shine like silver, I feel I've won
The battle I've fought within my mind
I've got rid of troubles, I've left them behind.

My mind is now empty as I soak in the peace
It's a wonderful way to find release
From pressures and stress, from pain and woe
That which I'm looking at is a picture on show.

It's placed in my mind like a large centrepiece
The CD I'm playing is continual, won't cease
It's 'Silver Wings' that can be heard
I lay there and listen to the sound of a bird.

The music it flows, the pictures so real
I know this is daft, but I can actually feel
The rays from the sun upon my face
And see the birds flying with such grace.

It's easy to switch off from the world in which we live
If it's just for a moment, we'd be able to sieve
That which matters and that which does not
So when we then stand, our worries are forgot.

I am a daydreamer and a proud one at that
For I find the peace even when I'm flat
Life has its problems, its ups and downs
But if we can relax, peace can be found.

We all should see how simple life can be
By looking for colour wherever we may be
It's easy to be down when thoughts go astray
But the trick is to relax and clear them away.

The Artist

The artist's skills are special gift
They bring in colour, which can lift
Any one person who is feeling down
The pictures painted remove a frown.

They paint the trees and birds up above
And are so inspired with hearts full of love
It's pleasure they give and joys abound
For watching them work is happiness found.

Their brush stroke displays care and compassion
They talk of forest, landscape or mansion
Their thoughts are away on a cloud so high
They sit for hours without having to sigh.

Their hands portray the talents of old
Where Elizabethan soldiers fought and were told
To follow orders come what may
The pictures on canvas they do then display.

Scenes from the past, both old and new
Life on Earth is hung up to view
However you may feel, in the gallery you'll find
History and interest for the artist is kind.

His views are in colour though some are chalked black
Those of the wars are for us to look back
And see that the scenes we can find ourselves in
Are wrong and unwanted for they are a sin.

Idealism can be theirs if in the right mood
But life as an artist can be harsh and quite crude
For money they have not, they may have to wait
To gain satisfaction knowing their work is top rate,

Which will hang in the homes of the gentry and such
Knowing their pictures are prized and loved much
But if fame is not theirs, they don't worry so
For they meet many people who are nice to know.

Isolation

When in isolation, thoughts can run deep
In the quietness of the hour when others are asleep
If one sits silently it is easy to hear
The sound of the wind is so very clear.

The sound of tree branches hitting the sill
Of an upstairs window, is a noise that can fill
One with fear if one's on their own
Isolation brings emptiness, making one groan.

For with no one to cuddle when feeling afraid
In an empty house, thoughts can wade
Into the deep; does anyone care
That we're alone and feeling despair?

The telephone is silent, the doorbell too
Why don't they ring, a visitor or two
Would be welcomed, does anyone see
When someone is sad and as lonely as can be?

By switching one's thoughts to what brings a smile
Can stop isolation for a short while
Everyone's busy in this world of ours
They go out dancing or driving fast cars.

Those that do not, stay in the home
They have no friends with whom they can roam
Choosing to stay secluded from most
In isolation, no one's their host.

Colleagues they have during their working day
But when evening approaches isolation can stay
Myself, I am happy with paper and pen
But understand those who pray for company,
Amen

Jealousy/Hate

Jealousy, hate, resentment or fear
That we have for others near
Will not bring comfort or make them kind
Get rid of it forever to get peace of mind
For this we can't have if we feel the great need
To curse those around us, instead of just feed
Them with love, showing that we care
If this were done, no enemies would be there
For they'd see that you love them and mean them no harm
Then friends you'd become, life would be calm
If all the world leaders thoughts about such
Then peace would be known and loved very much
By all in their countries, for what would be found
Is peace in the air covering the ground
It would be found in the hearts and minds of us all
So the people on Earth could stand very tall
For they'd have found the answer to everyone's prayer
And shown God above, that we really do care
About jealousy, hate, resentment and fear
I pray this will happen in time for next year.

School Playing Field

A summer's day, a glorious morn
Makes one feel it's great to be born
Upon the Earth with grass so green
Which is covered in daisies, it's a sight to be seen.

It lifts one's spirit, making one feel glad
That the Earth is a treasure and joy to be had
There's snowy white feathers blowing in the breeze
Along with some pollen which makes you want to sneeze.

Clearing our head and emptying our mind
Of any troubled thoughts, these are left behind
For it's hard to feel down and really quite grey
With God's gift of love and colour every day.

The broom on the hillside is the colour of sun
If thorns were not in it we could run and have fun
Through its swaying branches, but, they can do us harm
So we know to stay our distance but the colour brings calm.

The sunshine, the daisies, the grass and the broom
Bring one contentment not the feeling of doom
We can all feel real sad when wintertime is here
The trick is to appreciate any season of the year.

For nothing can harm us or cause us great pain
If we see life as beauty, long may it reign.

Problems

Life's little problems may get you down
But the trick is to ignore them or so I've found
For this way the dark clouds just disappear
Just imagine the light rays that fall around so near.

I sometimes dream of wonders to be
And forget all my problems that do worry me
There's no need to be sad or wear a long frown
For tomorrow's another day and they may not be around.

So if it's problems you have, just take my advice
And relax and find calmness, for you'll find life so nice.

Silver Skies

Silver skies and sea of blue
Gives you thoughts on what to do
A summer's day, an early morn
Brings a feeling that's cosy and warm.

The sun shining down, the sound of the waves
Seagulls chanting, it's easy to save
This moment forever within one's heart
Locked safely in there it never will depart.

The foam on the sand is a pleasure to see
Children play in it merrily
Washing their feet and being quite bold
Taking their clothes off but not getting cold.

There's a dog on the beach and starfish too
Sometimes they're yellow, but in water turn blue
The sight from the hillside that I sit upon
Brings in such joy, I could write it in song.

The clouds are of white with a silvery tinge
Looking at the horizon, it's just like a fringe
Hanging over the sea, which is a beautiful blue
Just picture the glory, it's a God-given view.

Weather/Whether

Weather and whether can be thought of the same
For when we're in doubt the clouds may bring rain
Whether this is done or that is said
Don't dwell, just remain
With calm thoughts and kindness
And thus, you'll stay sane.

To dither brings darkness like a dark winter's sky
To doubt brings confusion so you just wonder why
You wonder if whether
The day may bring grief
Please relax and find calmness
Thus, you'll find great relief.

Hole In The Ground

There's a hole in the ground I fall in a lot
It's there when life's smooth, but then goes to pot
For when I am happy, I think about woe
And how it just went, or where did it go?

It's something of a puzzle, then lo and behold
What I've been thinking about past days of old
Suddenly hits me afresh and anew
So really you could say I make myself blue.

For the hole's always there to place myself in
If I look for any sadness that's gone in the bin
I dig it all out so it's there to be found
Why couldn't I be happy with the joy that's around?

Instead I looked back with thought about the days
When darkness appeared and no calm bays
What I must do to put misery at rest
Is think about happy times, those I love the best.

Then maybe the hole that's there in the ground
Would eventually cease, no longer be found
Thus, I would not fall or find myself sad
And my life would be great and not sometimes bad.

Elena Tincu-Straton

Born in Tirgoviste, Romania, studied in Bucharest, Uxbridge and London. Now living in London. She is influenced by Romanian poets such as Eminescu, Blaga, Nichita Stanescu.

Her poems have appeared in magazines including 'Other Poetry', 'The Journal', 'Quantum Leap', 'Iota', 'First Time', 'Dandelion', 'Obsessed With Pipework', 'Decanto', 'Aireings', and in anthologies published by United Press and Anchor Books.

Snow

Hide with me among leaves. Show your face.
I wait for you there where I've never been.
You will find me there where I am no more.
For now I lower the 'us' into your hands,
die more and more in you, less in myself.
Earth will cover my mouth with its own,
yet I find peace inside the hunger.
I'll be soon among the things that have gone
but come back to you in summer,
and won't wish to die anymore.

Winter, A Cuckoo

High in trees, winter, a cuckoo, lays eggs in somebody else's nest,
winter about to become a queen of the winged kind.
There's silence until what is conceived is white.
Then the hatching, all the eggs at once, see these birds amazed
                                                                with flight,
these beaks between soft flappings? They've kept the white,
the fledglings, a tenderness of queens.
Winter running from field to field just to watch
secret love children grow at once with the wheat.
Winter always a trick ahead, letting the plant from underneath;
big birds gone, scared by what they cannot say.

Remember how it cried through us at the end,
and we both kneeled in the white confession, those wings swarming,
smudging my gaze the more I wanted to forget.
Remember how we all left with a heart made of water and stone
                                                                after that.

From All

From all that I've lost, from all that I have dreamed,
all that I plaited and has come undone,
from all that I've seen and have not felt,
from all that has dribbled out and I have not buried,
from all that has risen and yet it has not reached,

Oh God, make a wound to hurt the poppy
on the bread that feeds five thousand,
and drips between the sea that crushes my confinement
and the one continuing in hunger.

Elemental

Fire tells me with many tongues: you know so little about passion.
When fire begins, love follows.

Air fills me with many stars: you know so little about snow.
When snow begins, white follows.

Water tells me in whispers: you know so little of partings.
When water begins, sky follows.

Earth cradles me in graves: you know so little of arriving.
When I begin, fire follows.

Word

Oh, free me into the language into the deep of the language
where water has many names and the balance between
flowing and continuity is struck; give me
a torch, let me see the river that is inventing me.

Oh, free me into the language into the still of the language
where the reefs of the unspoken grow; let me find
the mouth that has love for the silent.

Only the fascination of the deep makes me rise so as
to put above what is underneath.

Counting

The gently touched skin, its just remembered 'me',
the slowness of hand as it leaves the 'you',
the hold's shallow root so that it escapes the 'we',
its scent of a rose that's closing its heart,
the south of the 'us' from where migration has begun,
the 'me' between your noes like a drum,
the silence lying with 'yes', the white of the snow elsewhere
because it's gentler on 'you's' like that,
its rush to lick footfalls so that it keeps the 'us',
the stubbornness of the road us it turns after almost saying 'they',
the stiffness of the night that gazed too long at you and
now lies in darkness, its blind wiping of the 'us'.

Is This?

Is this flight with birds homing south, your gaze?
This silence, the word becoming a thief?
Is this crocus spring pronouncing your name?
Is this horizon a love that doesn't know how to stop?
Is this poppy the 'me' that hasn't burned already?
Is this image in the mirror the betrayal of the moment as it lets go of us?
Is this line in my palm the story healing after it has gone through?
Is this light going, counting its years, us?
Is this oblivion the time we didn't have?
Is this ducking and diving of the gulls amidst lines, me?

What Is This?

What is this cut through me without hurting,
this beautiful bleeding with you,
this burning of my thousand skins,
what is this space with gulls expressing me as cry?
What is this wind blowing the candle of my words,
this weighing down of all my boughs,
this sideways fall of the head like that of a snowdrop?
What is this starting again of the lips?
What is this growing all night and shrinking at dawn with the dew,
those birds in me that don't spread wings as they don't know
if they're going to fly, these swans that don't sing as
they don't know if they're going to die?
What is this wash of ink for blood?

Summer, lower your head so I can still see him.
Not a sound as you go away, only the hour when we were young,
only the hour when we were beautiful.

Your Fingers

Your fingers directing birds, happy they're still homing,
that they still reach.
Your fingers practising the undulating rhythm of hills, holding irises.
Your fingers deftly choring on, peeling yourself, letting me be revealed.
Your fingers summoning angels without even knowing,
loved more by them empty like that.
Your fingers first to feel I'm near, saving the words like coins in a
motherly knot of your handkerchief.
Your fingers peaceful as they close the last gate, tenderly proving
dust beautiful.

Monday

The fire flows, moistens its lips,
the water burns, gives back the sky,
the body waters the land, the soul flying south,
the geese return becoming an eye,
the love rises on. Isn't it enough for a day?

Thesaurus

Wound is loving on the inside,
sunset is dying whilst still beautiful,
fire is the parting of the grape with the wine,
grave is the 'me' that takes longer to die,
soul is the margin between having done and what's left to do,
stone is the memory river carries and dumps,
ghost is a love that doesn't know its tomb,
repentance is the road turning back,
bulb is being awake after your time has died,
tomorrow's not the potter, tomorrow's the jug,
story is what word has stolen from me and given you.

Icarus

Hunger takes me to you; there are crumbs of you in the air,
I cannot eat and be without you.

Air is a thousand yous. I cannot breathe and be myself.

Heart, this hammer with my blood, breaks me into the four winds.
I cannot love and be whole.

Sky, a bird with my wings, flies me to you. What's down in me is high.
I cannot be horizon as I move dangerously with love.

What you know of me is flight, takes me past fear.
I cannot be sky as I learn how to fall

It's OK

As dusk silences you, I carry words to your mouth.
It's OK, Mama. I'm afraid too. The way you look at me and leave,
the way you turn away your head and come back.
But the yoke of time breaks and you pour the other way,
take the road under your tribe. Only in autumn I can feel your texture,
when all leaves are shed and fields start again, out of love.
You're now what you always were: a dream of becoming,
and clay moistens its lips as it tells you the choring's over,
you have earned the way back to yourself.

Love

I am this fire blazing, bursting all directions,
I feed my passion with my breast. Look at this flaming with myself.
I was taught by deserts, I understand thirst.
This burning of the sand as it parts with the water is
me living towards you. Impatient, I tell my secrets with my face.
I haven't got a language yet I can whisper anything.
Heart rages in me, comes out in thousands. By burning,
it gets back what it has lost. When I can't keep quiet,
I wander lands, melt forests. What you hear is your loss.
My flames in beautiful bodies, my touch wearing out no sky.
Rainbow is just obsession of my mind. I steal meaning from the ice.
Touch me. I am you. Will you ever be me?
When bile mixes with my wine, I feel it with a thousand hearts.
I let sadness beg and beg, caress with the underneath 'me'
which is there in the ash. This distance in my arms is
a strange desire to die, pass through gates, listen to ferrymen crossing.
Soon I will start snowing so as I won't be fragmented,
and the way I warmed you be preserved.

A Winter Tale

Her face remains soft as she leans to put dry logs into the stove,
the background of snow falling turning her eyes more into the kerosene
she pours over a handful of ashes, bent like that after
she builds the wooden pyramid above it and strikes the match,
the lowered hand steady afterwards. Fire hisses at her face,
silence hisses at her heart. She does not look for words,
language is a harder fire to build right now.
A few more twigs thrown in as if to wound this beautiful flame.
How empty coldness will be. I like that arching of her while
everything else is vertical. Snow falling. Snow falling harder as
she thinks there's enough to keep the fire going,
as she opens the door. Snow closes her eyes for her.
She still has that softness of the face on a street that
meanders heavily through snowdrifts that light the night ahead.

She did not return, mother, but the fire is still burning.
She went away to other fires, climbed hills where snow has soft lips
and wet whispers, where clay promises rest,
where time does not reach, time at a loss.

The Morning After Death

Wind opens all my doors, my amazement hides my face.
I split into a thousand pieces, broken light, finer and finer.
Air keeps changing me, I am no longer myself.
I am out of my mind with flight. I cannot be seen, only spoken.
Distance cannot hurt me anymore. See this horizon?
It's me holding onto my heart. I rise in my own flight,
I lost my earth but found the sky. I thought I was strong yet
I tremble with each breeze. I thought I was weak yet
I raised a stone behind. I am this air I don't know,
this place I've never been, the life in the silence
that is too strong to die, I dance with my heart,
not with my feet, like spring, awake all boughs.
This shine on them is me. On a day without wind
I fly towards the me in yourself. Hear this sound?
It's me keeping you in my heart. I'm approaching mystery,
can't understand now. I can only love.
Wind enters me to become a handful of dust.
All I have now from a lifetime is this flight.
Having left all of me behind, what it reaches is my love.
I am where wind has remembered to blow
and love has forgotten to die. I am everywhere.

Thawing

(i.m. Teodora Costeanu)

Covered by birds as if still in danger, my body,
brought out of the seas alive, lowers on the ground,
lets out two salivas: the white and the blue.
Loneliness right now is a beach which fills my mouth with seaweed.
How the birds force their way in me, stir me to flight,
revolt the image that's made from what I've lost.
So I need water to lead me to a sense of trust,
birds straining it with sounds that haven't forgotten anything.
I catch my breath, let myself be carried.
I'll be soon on the seas again: the should of the white,
the must of the frost, the will of the crossing.

Death

It lifts my veil like that of a bride, this big love that has come
only for me.
It must have me in order to be itself. The only veil that has me is me.
My heart does not open, only soaks with mystery,
remembers what winter teaches: closeness can kill.

It lifts my veil like that of a bride, it wants to live and be me.
The only me that has me is myself. My arms do not open,
go down like boughs, unconfessed, remember what winter teaches:
if you don't touch me you won't catch fire.

It lifts my veil like that of a bride; it must be cool in order to give itself,
I have to burn in order to take it. The only flame that has death is death.
My body does not open, remains a stranger under my veil,
knows that snow is the hesitation of the sky before journeying back.
I keep falling in this love. Together we become a winter.

Time Is A Gypsy

Time is a gypsy, never knows its true direction,
which wind. It claims no land; each night under the stars,
it sets traps and baits, opens the heads of vipers, knowing
how to wound. What it seizes is its truth.

It waits for me where I am not - my ruin is its splendour -
takes from me to make its own. Leaves these rags.
On my music it lifts my veil like that of a bride,
follows me into my bone, gives my name to a stone.
Silver is its sorcery with moon.

It has seen gods stiffen stones but no stones yet to stiffen gods,
felt that this day is not the whole autumn, that this love is not the
                                                    whole sky.
It looks at itself in coins. At dawn it juggles with fire almost being seen.

Sick of the world, its cart moves on rubber wheels, not a sound.
Its only witness is this road that echoes a travelling stillness
and proves nothing but rattles and smoke.

* * *

As my body, unable to return to the sky, curses the land
lying randomly, until a road takes pity;
as my breast was the first to meet the knife,
(I am a stone that stopped but so many others beat on)
as I've wanted something to remind me of you and got your youth,
(I am a hunter, remember? Throwing loops.)
you live towards me as I become you
no distance can stop us now.

Rain

I make the river, touch it with willows,
help it build its banks with what stones I have.
I know too about exile, no longer remember where I was born.
Gulls fly in me so they know how I sound.
I listen to everybody's heart, share secrets with the humble:
roots honour me above all others. I grow antlers like forests
and let the deer loose in them, tremble in the hoof mark;
I am the most fearful of the two. But most of all I come on
your hands as they move the stones, the shores, the boughs,
and tender the crocus they hold, give it a soul.
I pass through your fingers just to learn your body,
grow my hair just to touch your feet.
I am no water, I am only a flame.
When I don't exist for you anymore I come to lightning that
                                                    I might burn.
The sun picks me from broken shells until it imagines I am gone.
Love is the home of my last hour. I dig it and find my bones.

Land Of Coffins

In the small hut, silence walks with mother's steps;
it doesn't look who's entered, though feels it's me.
Time throws in a pebble, wrecks what silence is carrying,
keen of having back what belongs to it.
The laid table first: the dough left to swell,
you sit next to a coffin of bread. Egg shells having let go,
earthenware holding in, glass baring the light.
Time wanders outside, not knowing what it is
so that it depends on no one. Now the cleaning of the room
where you pause after feeling pain. You sit next to a coffin of speech.
Words fallen, their burden thrown away like that of a footmark.
Language now, a lonelier place. The pyramid of logs above
a handful of ashes that smell of kerosene follows, this coffin of wood.
Only ash holds what's precious, you get closer to the fire,
your margins gathered in a tear just waiting to fall.
The long row of chores first, mother. Then all the rest.
Time lowers me in your imprint so that you can rise and be free.
But first of all the chores, mother. Then the hearse.

Francis Hughes

I was born in Dublin, Eire and that was several bright moons ago. I have spent most of my adult life in Luton, Bedfordshire.

When I first arrived here from Ireland, I was a very happy young man. Happy at my place of work, happy at home and happy when out socialising.

A few years ago that villain depression entered my soul and almost succeeded in destroying me. I fought back with the help of a professional body and a good woman also helped me, and she of course, is my dear wife. 'Twas then I decided to express myself on paper and I haven't stopped since.

I had my first poem published in a London Journal some years ago and that gave me a lot of confidence. Then I had my work accepted in Poetry Now and Spotlight Poets and was fortunate enough to have two of my poems make it into 'The Top 100 Poets'.

I also indulge in long work and am ashamed to admit I neglected my poetry through this. However, I've rectified that and it won't happen again.

In previous profiles, I expressed why I decided to become a vegetarian, which was several years ago and from that to a vegan. I love animals and loath those so-called humans whom ill-treat them. Another thing I cannot understand is why Christians seem to ignore the 5th Commandment! Which means 'all living creatures'. Thus every Christian should be a vegetarian, at least!

A Board Of Poker Players

A professor,
A psychiatrist,
A barrister
And a doctor

sat around the table
playing a shrewd game
of poker with the intentions
of bluffing me.

The game lasted over ten hours
while they scored points in
favour of the dead men, and deducted
more than plenty on me.

When they failed
to score me zero!
They threw in their hands
and awarded me redress.

This City

This city
with its beauty and ugliness;
Georgian houses and squares
and squalid squats!
Cathedrals, some open
others closed like prisons,
broken in half
by a river with many bridges.

This river, with its dive-splashing minnow
and the magic of the musical sounds
from those places that once controlled a naive race
where they claim to change wafer and wine
into body and blood;
such a fantastic claim
turns mine to wax.

Nowadays quite a percentage of the population
are living a lucrative lifestyle
with Euros growing in their plots!
The honest and the dishonest
are living the life of Riley.
Proletarians living in houses
fit for stockbrokers . . .

The students of celibacy are hoarse
from screaming into deaf ears;
and their fire and brimstone has turned to ice.
Their establishments used to be full to the brim
on the Sabbath and other holy days of obligation;
but now they are as empty as a dunce's head
in this capital city.
But in rural areas nothing has changed
for fear of the collar.
And after the mighty Nelson
was blown from his pillar;
he should have been replaced by the immortal Saint Brendan
opposed to a metal monstrosity
pointing toward the naked sky
which is a laughing stock
to structural engineering;
and to the widest street in Europe.

Replacements

Contemporary verse
replaced rhyme.

The farm tractor
replaced the horse.

The bullet
replaced the spear.

The internet
replaced conciliation.

Unemployment
replaced happiness.

Maggie Thatcher
replaced witchcraft;

And Tony Blair
replaced socialism.

The Master Duke

The Duke was sadistic
arrogant and vile.
Paced the classroom
like a bald panther;
and when really vexed
the veins stood high
on the back of his neck
like railway tracks,
and then he'd chant!
'You ignorant bastards,
when you leave school
join Jim Larkin's Union
and get your bread and butter free.'
When I reported him to my dad;
he kicked Duke in the three-piece suite
and Duke was on the sick for a month.
So too was I the day before he retired.

Apathy

Who cares?
They don't.
The enemy
of the working class.
As lazy as park benches.
Voting should be compulsory.

They sharpen my blunt knife
When they blatantly wheel
The House of Commons
into the pubs'
and preach politics.
The hypocrites.

See him over there
with the big head?
He's a Tory you know;
The same judgmental bastards
never bother to journey
to the polling station.

When miserable winter
arrives on their doorstep;
I wonder
will they be honest enough
to refuse
the cold weather payment?

Desperate Fran

For several years
he was a clown;
an unpaid circus clown
staggering about town

riding the oblivion train
and oblivious
to which station
that train would terminate.

Residing in cloud cuckoo land
and always leaving behind him
a trail of broken glass
without breaking any windows.

Continued to struggle along
that self destructive trail
with loose burning tongue
spitting verbalised fire

until blind eyes could see
the colours of the rainbow;
then decided once and for all
to cash in on a miracle.

Proper Bastards

Very good at hiding it
for several wily years
you saucy bedroom lepers

and still able to criticise others
for their antisocial behaviour while
you are busy cremating your vows

in the burning flames of lust.
You swapped your gold for brass
to lie with your bit on the side.

You also lie through the enamel
of your false laughing teeth when
you blow sweet kisses to your kids

when they leave the house for school.
They, oblivious to your capers destroying
this precious institution, and hopefully
they will learn the difference
between loyalty and deception;
unlike you. Proper bastards.

She's Stuck In The Past

She's stuck in the past
cradling her pride
without swallowing it;
and when in the wrong

an apology is a swear word.
She juggles her thoughts
through the air of yesteryear
while wiping the cold blood

from the blade of her blunt knife
as she travels alone through space
agog waiting for the important story
that could put her on another planet.

And oh so eager watching for changes
on the stock exchange
while choking on a stick of dynamite
and declaring war on the passive!

The Tempest

The tempest
blows wild
at the drop
of a hat.

'Tis stormy
years old
from the time
I was a boy.

This blowing
wild storm
can only
be calmed

The sunny day
when I manage
to lasso a sweet
gentle breeze.

The Elephants Whom Never Forget

Chips on their shoulders
like logs on an open fire,
burning and smouldering away
their memories of yesteryear.

Disturbing their brain cells
then hammering away at -
what used to be
opposed to what is now.

One drunk of yesteryear
but now a reformed character
and the lesson was expensive;
was subjected to a slimy comment

I have no time for that poet
I remember him when! -
So comrades be very wary of those
elephants whom never forget.

Animosity

Animosity stinks
as strong as
farmyard dung.

'Tis still fresh
in the front
of your minds

like your weekend
shopping list.
Still you try

to hide it
while pretending
to forgive and forget!

Though subjected to zero tolerance;
forgiveness is worthless;
unless you can forget . . .

Julie Rutherford

I have worked in the theatre as a stage manager with companies ranging from the Royal Shakespeare Company to west end musicals including the first British production of 'Annie'. I have written two plays, 'Laura' and 'Affinities'.

'Final Parting' was the first of a series of works intended for musical performance and it was set to music, and first performed in 1996 alongside Faure's Requiem. 'Towards The Light', a song cycle triptych is currently being set to music by the Austrian composer Norbert Zehm; the Polish composer George Maievsky, and the English composer Graeme Hopson. Dorian Kelly has set a jazz version.

2004 saw the completion of 'Cantio Animae' an oratorio; a second song cycle 'Winter, When Past Unseen', and two further song cycles 'Beyond The Horizon' and 'A Wanderer's Lament'.

A number of poems from the cycles have been and are due to be published in the poetry magazines 'Rubies In The Darkness', 'Littoral', 'Earth Love', 'Time Haiku', 'Poetry Church', 'Decanto', 'Carillon', and in a poetry anthology 'Our Moment In Time'.

I write poetry because I feel an emotional need to express myself and to explore what I feel and think. My influences are music, love and nature. The recurrent themes are a search for spiritual meaning, which I explore through love, loss, pain and nature - travelling as I do on a geographical and spiritual journey through the cycle of poems, (or a conscious/unconscious journey) in an attempt to try and feel God's presence, somewhere, in all things.

There are no answers - I do not have any. What I try to express is a journey we all make in our lives - I try to make some sense of it.

Towards The Light (Part 1)

*'How selfhood begins with a walking away
and love is proved in the letting go . . . ' Cecil Day Lewis*

*Hokusai wave
            crescendo . . .

listen . . .
            calm sea
                gentle, lapping sound

take this moment now

let me lay my head
on your shoulder

for tomorrow you will be gone

 *Image based on the print 'the hollow of the
  deep-sea wave off Kanagawa' by Hokusai

Untitled

Go then and leave me with 'the sonnets'
and speak no more of love
wretched, wretched nights
of shattered dreams
wrestling spirit
your face haunting me; constant

trembling, shaking, distracted,
fevered, frenzy of love,
how could you do it?
how could you be so cruel
to leave me with this unknowing , , ,
     this damned misery
     this agonising despair

go then, depart Sir
and to India be gone
far easier to love at a distance
than not to love at all

Away, Alone

Still water,

      silent mountain

      a ripple
         a quiver

      a moment
         gone

Go Away

Leave me
let me be gone
where I can escape the tyranny
of your conflicts
and the turbulence
of my own mind and soul
it is not a quiet love
but wracked by demons
of your past and mine

sad it is, yes sad
that we have looked love in the eye
and felt the heart flutter
with such high hope and joy
but those black demons down under
keep us apart
pray Sir, do not torment me
with your sweet looks, your loving eyes
my heart is bitter, my heart cries

Untitled

See there,
      how the swan flies

with grace,
      so serene,
         above the reeds

gentle, lapping
      sound of the water

ripples,
      reverberate

Untitled

Like an anchored weight
my mind, my heart, my soul
lies on the ocean floor
unable to breathe . . .
seeking only the ideal of love
from behind closed bars
love, that has turned in on itself
becoming a tyrannical force
negative in its ways . . .

sweet freedom
white light
beckoning, on the horizon
always I have searched for you
yearning, yearning, in vain
to be set free
from servitude,
the final,
       letting go

Untitled

Listen,
> to the shifting cloud

> to the mountain,
>> the mist descending

listen,
> to the sea
>> to the wave break gently on the shore

>> to the wind rustle in the trees
>>> to the falling leaf

listen,
> to the running brook

> to the skylark,
>> sing,
>>> the curlew, cry

Sanctus Spiritus (Part II)

(For Andrew)

For our souls are blown through the winds of time . . .

'Listen . . .
do you hear me?'
                    the bird sings,
'then, I did . . . ' I reply

how the beauty struck me . . .
tired, I walk down
into the wood . . .
trying to find some peace
from those anguished thoughts,
                        of love . . .

this deer's footprint . . .
that blade of grass -
the way the light flickers
through the pine trees,
                    there . . .

solitude,
            and silence,

I embrace,

                and let nature's spirit speak
                once more,
                    to my hungry soul . . .

Untitled

Shun not the light,
the clouds are breaking
on this darkness . . .
lift up your heart
and with that your mind
for the two
not inseparable,
are entwined -
let go,
      and breathe
an intake of new life
see there, the clouds are shifting
and now,
      a shaft of sunlight
transitory yes,
but enough, for a moment,
that all shadows cease
brief moment of hope
                  pray, stay

Untitled

evening

mist falling,
       wind rustles in the trees

       babbling brook
          swiftly gathers pace

      spider scrambles with a fly

night falling,

        falls,

buzzard cries,

        a fretful cry

Mater Dolorosa

From
        this darkness
I lift up my eyes
            to see,
                beyond the visible

I lift up my hands
        for your silent touch

for with you
there are no secrets, no boundaries
                        no hidden thoughts

you see my blemished soul
and your love,
                surpasses all earthly limits

now, in this silent moment
in your presence
I stand before you,

                    alone

Is God In The Marshes?

On the marshes,
in the darkness,
before
        dawn breaks,
a bird takes to flight,
a cock crows,
an owl calls out,
water gently
                laps,
sounds
        echo
                In the silence,
reverberate
        against each other
in this empty place

someone asked me if I felt God there
why there?
why not here, in my lounge
or,
        in the monastery on the Downs

God! ask another . . .
or ask God if he is here, or there
                        or wherever,

you'll hear silence . . .
and, maybe in that silence
a cock will crow,
or an owl
        might call out

Lamentation

The wind
      sighs, knowingly
         through the trees

clouds swiftly pass by
I hear the murmur of the mountain stream
the swallows . . .

        where have they gone?

In the autumn wind,

        I feel your goodbye

Sanctus Spiritus

Lord, I ask
remove this turmoil from my heart
and unwanted thoughts from my head
that lead me astray
Lord, I ask
turn all my fear into love

Lord, I ask
fill my head and heart with
peace and silence
Lord, I ask
that I may stay close to you
in stillness and love,

come,
        Holy Spirit
            come

Evening Lamentation (Part III)
Dawn

(In memory of my friend, Sidney Jowers)

Under this lonely mountain

white clouds,
                    linger
                            mist lies low

gentle rain,
                    falls
trees,
            drip with the morning dew

                    fledgling,

                    alone
                    on a branch

wind sighs . . .

                    a sorrowful lament

Lonely Waters

Still,
      and calm the water . . .

mute swan
      silently,   glides

            gentle breeze
            lightly upon my cheek

sad memory
      of love,

        dying

Untitled

You will remember this in time to come
that I loved you once
                          and now it's gone

you will remember this in time to come
the way I looked at you
and how my eyes sang with such sweet joy
                          and now that's gone

you will not remember this in time to come
of how my heart
ached, with such sad pain
for I never let you see my love,
                          die within

Untitled

Spirit

    moves

        as the shadow
           swiftly crosses

              the mountainside

        as the chill
           harsh wind
              cries
                through the trees

       solitary kestrel

       hovers . . .

       above its prey

          before
            the final swoop

Untitled

Two birds,
             sit on an acacia branch

the mountain fades
              away
                into the dusk,

             into the
                silence of the night

in the stillness,

      a lone bat

        cries

Ron Beaumont

I was born in the cathedral city of Truro in 1934, the youngest of five children of whom only my two elder brothers and myself are still living. My parents were by no means well off, but I don't remember ever being hungry or without adequate clothing. I attended the Redruth County Grammar School. Upon leaving there I more or less just drifted through life, working my way through numerous jobs which, if they had any prospects at all, were never seized upon by me.

While at school, my best subject was always English, so I suppose that was where my love of poetry germinated; although having 'played around' with writing verse myself I did nothing positive about it until 1995, since which time I have had numerous poems published by Forward Press, and in Spotlight Poets in 2003. At one time I was writing poems for a gentleman named Ray Shaddick who had a programme on BBC Radio Cornwall. These poems were about various events taking place in Cornwall, ie: Helston Flora, Royal Cornwall Show, Tall Ships Race, The Eclipse, etc. I write poetry because I find it relaxing, and basically I quite simply enjoy doing it.

My inspiration is provided by most anything at all, and I attempt to encompass, if possible, all human emotions. Poems are also written for and about friends, but since these are purely personal, and produced as an appreciation of their friendship, they are never submitted to publishers.

If there is a 'recurrent theme' to my work, it is more than likely that the theme is love. I have always been an incurable romantic.

Apart from my poetry, my other interests are Native American Culture and collecting United States Law Enforcement Badges and Patches.

On Reading Wordsworth

On reading famous works poetic,
Some mournful, some in love enshrined,
Some introspective, some prophetic,
Bring quite tangential thoughts to mind.
I ponder on the author's view
Of that on which his eyes alight -
And does he ask, as I would do
'. . . Is this the truth of which I write . . . ?'
When Wordsworth's 'Daffodils' I read,
Irreverent though my thought may be
It raised this question in my head
Which ever more will nag at me.
I wondered if the lonely cloud
'That floats on high o'er vales and hills'
Grew weary of that 'golden crowd'
So rained upon those daffodils,
And with its torrents beat them down
Until at last the damn things drowned.

Red Angels

(An appreciation of Native American women)

Her tanned satin skin has a 'Black Hill's Gold' lustre;
Her raven's-wing hair any woman would prize.
In obsidian eyes little prairie stars cluster.
She can take life head on, and with no compromise.
Her bearing, befitting of any princess
Make the Sioux justifiably proud of their own,
As their 'White Painted Woman', the Apache no less
Imbue her with powers no other has known.
Crow woman, renowned for her exquisite beading
Can often herself be a rare work of art;
For none who have seen her could pass by unheeding,
Or ignore that quick beat of desire in their heart.

Assiniboine woman is gracefully regal;
Navajo woman stands stately and proud.
Gros Ventre woman is swift as the eagle;
Each of them clearly stands out in a crowd.
Lakota Sioux woman rules - Queen of the Plain.
Somehow their presence transforms the mundane.

Inherent Audacity

Did you ever in your life take time to cast a questing eye
Over your perception of yourself, and recognise a lie?
The lie we English all hold dear, '. . . our way is right . . .' we preach,
'. . . Other races need our guidance . . .', so their cultures we'd
impeach.
The seeds of self-destruction dwell in all of humankind.
Some dormant stay, but others may in dark thoughts be enshrined.
They will germinate unbidden, until that fateful hour
When they'll override morality, and burst forth into flower.
It's then we start to castigate the lifestyle of another.
Ours, we say, is life's true way. Invalid, any other.
By what right do we judge, in haste, those we don't understand?
Men's cultures are their heritage, entrenched in their homeland.
And just because they differ from beliefs that we hold strong,
It doesn't mean supremacy is ours, and they are wrong.
Since time primeval, in this world, blind bigotry's been rife.
Look deep within yourself and ask, *'. . . am I the cause of strife?'*

A Loafer's Lament

Who invented mornings, does anybody know?
And if you do, please tell me - I'll shoot the so-and-so.
I'm tucked up warm and comfy in my cosy little bed,
Then suddenly it's morning, it's doing in my head.
I'm not a 'mornings' person, they're all too much for me.
They're simply not conductive to harmonious dormancy.
Whilst poets praise the morning with its 'rosy-fingered dawn',
I view it with a jaundiced eye, dejected and forlorn.
So, who invented mornings? I really wish I knew.
I'd tie him to the nearest tree and beat him black and blue.
I'd make him curse his day of birth and torture him until
He'd learned one vital lesson:
Let this sluggard loaf at will!

Repose

A stray November sunbeam fluttered idly through the window,
As though seeking refuge from the autumn chill.
And it settled on the counterpane of one sick, ageing patient -
One of many 'midst the elderly and ill.
While it rested there at length, it seemed to give the old man strength,
For he stirred, and opened wide his misty eyes.
As he gazed around the room, he perceived beyond the gloom
That reprise of life that made him realise
Of the many years he'd had, all the good ones and the bad,
Every one had moments filled with love and laughter.
There'd been battles fought and won, but now the time had come
For his journey to a just reward hereafter.
Of regrets he had but few, and he knew what he must do -
He sank back and closed his eyes with scarce a moan.
On his sickbed, frail and grey, all life's pain ebbed swift away,
And the sunbeam took his hand to lead him home.
But the old man stirred once more, and although his speech was poor
He addressed the sunbeam, trembling and slight.
He said, 'Okay sport, I'm ailing, but your eyesight must be failing,
It's not my turn, it's that poor bloke on my right.'
But the sunbeam's swift reply was to just transmogrify
Into something like a chain, link upon link -
Wrapped itself around his throat until the poor old fellow choked
'Not your turn yet mate?
That's what you bleedin' think.'

The School Reunion

It's our good old school reunion and, as memories flood back,
Half-remembered names and faces, is that fat man really Jack?
He always used to look so suave, he dressed with style and flair -
But now he's turned into a slob, no longer debonair.
And the woman that he's married to, her pinched and pallid face
Looks uncomfortably familiar; oh my God! It's 'easy Grace'!

There's a bleached blonde in the corner putting on superior airs,
But we all know what her background is so no one really cares
As she boasts of her possessions, and her fancy house and car -
Her old Reliant Robin's parked outside some sleazy bar.
She says her home is 'listed eighteenth-century habitat';
But that's just a euphemism for a grotty council flat.

I see Peter Hume sometimes in town, he always gives a wave.
The conceited little poser thinks all women for him crave.
He drives a purple sports car, at a quite alarming pace,
With his glossy patent-leather hair, not one wisp out of place.
Rumour has it that his wife is both intelligent and trim,
But she can't be all that smart if she has wed a prat like him.

There's some damned enormous woman talking of 'our past', and yet
To my sure and certain knowledge we have never ever met.
She gushes, 'Dear, remember when . . . ?' I bleakly nod my head
Trying vainly not to show her that I wish that I were dead.
Choking back involuntary screams, I let her ramble on,
While I wonder who the hell she is, and where she knows me from.

Conspicuous by their absence are the famous brothers Vale.
The last I heard of them, they both were languishing in gaol.
Their criminal career it seems was not a great success -
They'd been caught shoplifting knickers in our local M&S.
Stealing women's lacy underwear, for reasons yet unknown,
Has us speculating if its use was meant for them alone.
There are some people here whose friendship I shall always treasure -
The ones who made the times we shared together such a pleasure.
They're the ones who stood beside you, we were mates through
                                        thick and thin,

To protect each other's backs, whatever trouble we were in.
Those who tried to come between us, soon would find to their dismay
They had a tiger by the tail, and that quite simply didn't pay.

Our head teacher, 'Dizzy' Durkin, something of a martinet,
Gave most every pupil nightmares, and memories linger yet
Of the many, many times I held my hand out for the cane,
As the fear of 'Dizzy's' strong right arm would paralyse the brain
With the most severe of punishments for those who broke the rules -
Medusa's head was never as repulsive as our school's.

There were those we liked and those we hated; some we just ignored;
Those who left us feeling good, and those who, frankly, left us bored.
I wish I'd never come tonight, I'll never come again -
I'd been looking forward to it, but now it's just a pain.
For although my thoughts are mixed about old classmates that I see,
I cannot help but wonder, *how are they now judging me?*

Phenomenal Light Show

(Remembering Cornwall's total eclipse of 1999)

And suddenly, the birds will cease their singing
as darkening shadows fall across the sun
the flower's petals close in supplication
total eclipse has wondrously begun
the opalescent moon will shield the county
from he who gives the world its warmth and light
changing the plants and animals' behaviour
when day turns inexplicably to night
the moon will emphasise the sun's corona
its rim accented by celestial fire
then, for a space of no more than three minutes
all light shall be extinguished - shall expire
and we, who if the sun were lost forever
would perish in a dark and cheerless void
stand watch, perhaps in fear and trepidation
that life could be so easily destroyed
those thousands who in wonder came to witness
will leave with memories none can forget
enthralling future wide-eyed generations
with tales of when both sun and moon paths met
such spectacle of nature's awesome power
will live forever in the minds of men
those few brief moments in a person's lifetime
before the sun reclaimed its sky again

Insanity

She's living deep within herself
No outward signs of life
No words express her inner thoughts
Beset by mental strife
No more that bright-eyed lovely girl
I'd courted in my youth
Then married in a perfect world
Of beauty, love and truth
For jealousy destroyed our love
It drove me to extremes
Until one night I killed a friend
(I still can hear her screams)
She had never been unfaithful
But in a drunken rage
I'd thought my friend her lover
Thoughts that nothing could assuage
For my best friend was my best friend
Just that, and nothing more
But jealousy within me grew
A festering, cankerous sore
I'd always been possessive
But now, I'd lost control
I killed him, and destroyed her mind
She'll never more be whole
She's living deep within herself
And knows far greater hell
Than I, who must live out my life
In this bleak prison cell

Cheyenne - Sioux - And Soldier Blue

Your thick flannel jacket is salt-rimed with sweat
You have been forty days in the saddle
Thirty miles every day, and you're unaware yet
Of your fate in the forthcoming battle
There's a long-barrelled Cavalry Colt at your side
And a single shot Springfield carbine
They've been bumping against you throughout the long ride
To a place that the world will headline
You are carrying twelve pounds of oats for your horse
Plus your Springfield and Colt ammunition
And oppressively merciless heat makes you curse
Those responsible for your condition
At the head of your column, in buckskin arrayed
Rides a General, hell bent on glory
But the annals of history soon to be made
Will record a formidable story
For the Cheyenne and Sioux will humiliate you
You'll be outflanked, outnumbered, outfought
Renown's flame won't warm you, nor that triumph ensue
Your vainglorious leader has sought
You will need this June day 1876, all the courage and strength
                                            you can muster
When the Little Big Horn becomes your River Styx
For your leader is George Armstrong Custer.

Weather Wise

Do you rail against our weather?
Do you curse our wind and rain?
Do you think that we're hard done by?
Pause a while, and think again.

Have we faced the dread tsunami?
Do you think we ever will?
When our weather's at its worst,
Well just how many would it kill?

What do we know of the hurricane,
Volcanoes or the quake?
Does our weather leave us total
Devastation in its wake?

No, we're relatively lucky weather-wise,
And though we moan,
Nature in her wildest moments,
Leaves us pretty much alone.

Just be grateful that our climate,
Even though it's not the best,
Doesn't have the power to lay
A whole community to rest.

The (Safe At Home) Front Line

While shrapnel-shredded corpses lie
In grotesque postures on some foreign beach
The politicians, safe at home
All glibly quote '. . . once more unto the breach . . .'
Do they know putrefaction's smell?
Those power-hungry men who sacrifice
The lives of those who live that hell
The ones compelled to pay their master's price
Their 'front line' takes them door to door
For obscene power to sacrifice yet more
A 'war of words' is all they wage
Their weapons, clichéd lies meant to assuage
And leech-like thrive on others' blood
They never once trudge ankle-deep in mud
Or tread some beach's blood-soaked sand
That witnessed their death's gruesome saraband
Where countless heroes their lives gave
When scything gunfire sent them to their grave
Those wielding power o'er life and death
Abuse that power with every fetid breath
Had they to take up arms and fight
They'd sue for peace, and whine about their plight

Summer Stock

As the curtain rises on another season
Spring's prologue, having set the scene, departs
Leaving Summer centre stage to woo the critics
And take her place in our responsive hearts

For Dame Summer's role is magically scripted
Bright rainbow hued her scenery and sets
It's a show of lazy days, of love and laughter
With chorus lines of starry-eyed coquettes

Directed and produced by a fêted master
The cast choreographed by life itself
Its audience, more than interactive extras
Reap the rewards of Mother Nature's wealth

Summer's worldwide tour performs to packed out houses
Though inspirational, too brief her stay
When that curtain falls, while memories will linger
We yet would wish a year-long matinee.

Spotlight Poets Information

We hope you have enjoyed reading this book - and that you will continue to enjoy it in the coming years.

If you are interested in becoming a Spotlight Poet then drop us a line, or give us a call, and we'll send you a free information pack.

Alternatively if you would like to order further copies of this book or any of our other titles, then please give us a call or visit our website at www.forwardpress.co.uk

Spotlight Poets

Spotlight Poets Information
Remus House
Coltsfoot Drive
Peterborough
PE2 9JX

Telephone: 01733 898102

Email: spotlightpoets@forwardpress.co.uk